J
729
ST

Storm, Betsy

I can be an
interior designer

$12.60

DATE			
SE 25 '91	JY 03 '02		
OC 30 '91	OC 5 '02		
AG 13 '92	AP 03 '03		
AP 29 '93	AP 22 '03		
JA 17 37	NO 14 03		
JE 2 '99	JE 28 04		
JY 24 00			
JA 18 '02			
FE 04 '02			
AP 01 '02			
JE 26 '02			

© THE BAKER & TAYLOR CO.

I CAN BE AN
INTERIOR DESIGNER

By Betsy Storm

Prepared under the direction of Robert L. Hillerich, Ph.D.

CP CHILDRENS PRESS®

CHICAGO

Library of Congress Cataloging—in—Publication Data

Storm, Betsy.
  I can be an interior designer / by Betsy Storm.
    p.   cm.
  Includes index.
  Summary: Describes the varied jobs of the interior decorator,
including talking with clients and working with color, light, and
space to create rooms in homes, office buildings, hotels, and
restaurants.
  ISBN 0-516-01958-9
  1. Interior decoration—Vocational guidance—Juvenile literature.
(1. Interior decoration. 2. Occupations.) I. Title.
NK2116.S76 1989
729'.023—dc20   89-15758
                                                CIP
                                                AC

Childrens Press®, Chicago
Copyright ©1989 by Regensteiner Publishing Enterprises, Inc.
All rights served. Published simultaneously in Canada.
Printed in the United States of America.
1 2 3 4 5 6 7 8 9 10 R 98 97 96 95 94 93 92 91 90 89

PICTURE DICTIONARY

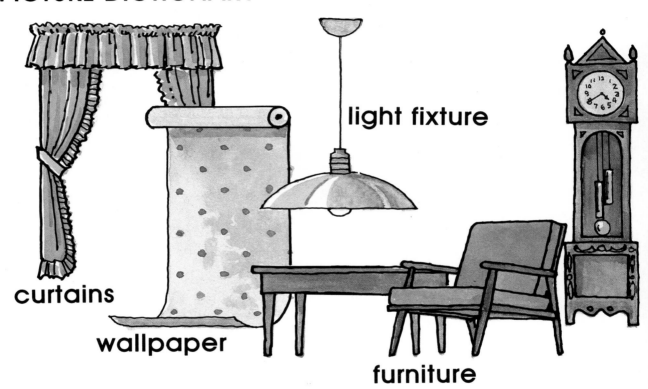

curtains

wallpaper

light fixture

furniture

playroom

workroom

sketches

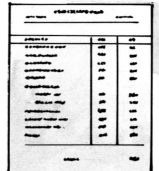

budget

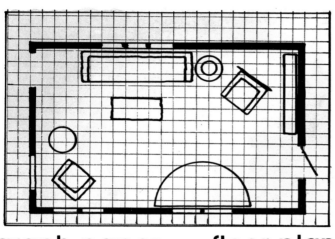

graph paper   floor plan

paint chips

clients

interior designer   design board

Did you ever dream of having a bedroom that looks like a castle in a fairy tale? How about a playroom that could pass for a spaceship?

playroom

Interior designers could make your dream come true. These people know how to take an empty room and change it into almost anything you might imagine.

interior designer

Interior designers love to
design beautiful living
spaces. They like to
create homes and offices
that suit the people who
live and work there. They
know how to match the

colors for walls and
furniture. They understand
how to arrange furniture in
a room.

furniture

Many people want to
make their homes more
modern or attractive.

An interior designer shows her client some pictures
of home interiors to help her decide on a new home design.

clients

workroom

They hire interior designers to help them. People who hire interior designers are called clients. Sometimes clients need to add closets or a workroom to their home. They may

8

This interior designer is checking to see how wallpaper will look next to curtains and floor coverings.

want new curtains or wallpaper.

curtains

wallpaper

Interior designers try to understand what their clients need. They ask many questions about the family that lives in the house. What are their favorite colors? What activities will take place in different rooms? A good interior designer is also a good listener.

Interior designers ask how much money the client wishes to spend. Then they plan how the money will be spent. This is called making a budget.

budget

The real work begins after interior designers

Top: A client looks at samples of furniture fabric.
Left: A designer confers with his client by
phone.
Above: Using photographs and a building's floor
plan, two interior designers work out some
design problems.

Look at all the home furnishings that have been chosen for this office (above) and living room (opposite page).

decide how a room
should look. Then they
know what kinds of home
furnishings are needed.
Home furnishings are all
the objects that go inside
a house or office.

Furniture, lamps, and even
paintings are some
examples of home
furnishings.

Sometimes clients have

A room might be designed around a client's favorite piece of furniture, such as a four-poster bed (left) or a *chaise longue* (right).

a favorite piece of furniture they want to keep. The designer then plans the room so that this piece fits in.

Interior designers always remember what their clients like and don't like.

Interior designers do a lot of work on paper. They make sketches and then detailed drawings to show what a room will look like when it's finished. Graph paper is used to show how things will be placed in relation to each other. A client looks at the drawings and approves them.

sketches

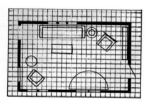

graph paper

Above: A designer at her drawing board. Below left: A designer's detailed drawing of a room. Below right: Checking materials against a floor plan

Left: A designer and client match up paint chips with floor tiles. Behind them hang hundreds of paint chips.
Right: A family looks at paint and wallpaper samples.

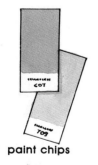

paint chips

Paint chips are small pieces of paper with different colors on them. Clients look at them to decide what color the walls should be. Wallpaper books show hundreds of

Drawing a floor plan

different wallpapers. An
interior designer and a
client look at these
together. Then they
decide what they like.

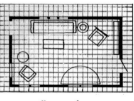

floor plan

The interior designer's
last step is to make a floor
plan. This is the final

19

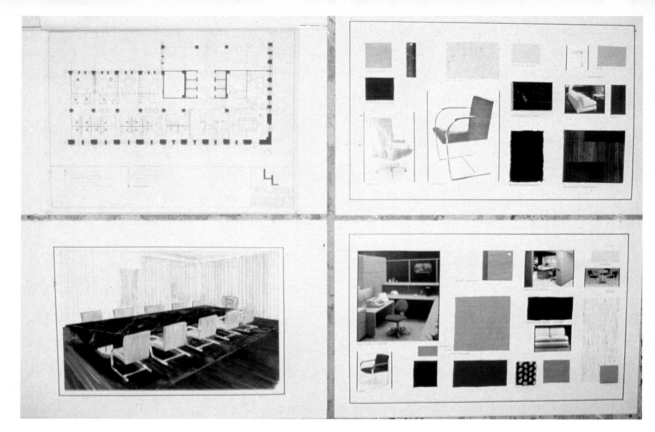

Design board for an office space, showing floor plan, furniture, carpeting, wall coverings, and other materials

design board

drawing that shows how a completed room will look. Another important tool is the design board. This board shows samples of furniture and curtain fabric, carpeting, and paint colors.

20

If the client likes the floor plan and the design board, purchases are made and the work begins. The purchases might include new light fixtures, new carpets, or new furniture.

light fixture

Sometimes interior designers are called decorators. Decorating is the part of their job that involves color and the way things look. But interior designers are concerned with more than just looks. They want the space inside a house to be useful, too. This might mean adding a room or having special furniture made.

Upper left: A room that blends many vivid colors
Above: A space designed for several different activities
Left: Furniture specially made for a particular room

23

Interior designers work in different places and on many kinds of projects. Some work in department stores or furniture stores. Others specialize in designing offices, hotels, or restaurants.

Interior designers need a good background in many areas. They must know about building and decorating materials. They must also understand how color affects people.

Many interior designers go to college. Some go to special schools for interior design or art. They study design, art history, furniture styles, and architecture. But some successful designers don't go to college. They learn on the job. In some states, interior designers must get a license to work in that state.

Above: Classroom in a design school
Right: Students at a design exhibit
Lower right: Drawing a floor plan as a
class assignment
Below: Student designers looking at
samples

Are you excited by color and what it can do? Do you notice if a room looks interesting and feels comfortable? Maybe you would like to be an interior designer.

Interior designers are problem solvers. They like

Interior designers love helping people to enjoy their homes.

to pay attention to details. Helping people enjoy their homes makes them feel proud. Interior designers especially like to hear people say, "You've done a wonderful job—the room looks beautiful!"

WORDS YOU SHOULD KNOW

architecture (AR • ki • tek • shur)—the study of designing buildings

attractive (uh • TRAK • tiv)—pleasing to look at

budget (BUD • jet)—a plan for spending a certain amount of money

clients (KLY • ents)—customers; those who buy someone's services

fabric (FAB • rik)—cloth

floor plan (FLORE PLAN)—the drawing of a room that shows the size and shape of the floor and the objects that will be on the floor

graph paper (GRAF PAY • per)—sheets of paper with lines going up and down and across, so that the sheets are covered with squares

home furnishings (HOME FUR • nish • ings)—objects that go inside a house, such as curtains, lamps, paintings, furniture, and light fixtures

interior (in • TEER • ee • ur)—the inside of something; the outside is the "exterior"

license (LY • sens)—official permission to do something

light fixtures (LITE FIX • churz)—devices on ceilings or walls that hold light bulbs or other light sources

sketches (SKECH • iz)—rough drawings

wallpaper (WALL • pay • per)—a decorative wall covering made of paper or cloth

INDEX

About the Author
  Betsy Storm is a former magazine editor. She now works as a free-lance writer and editor and has a special interest in family issues, consumerism, and law. Several years ago, Ms. Storm and a partner owned and operated their own custom chocolate company. She lives in Wilmette, Illinois, with her children, Kate and Colin.